HEADS UP !
by Randy G. Roy

Published by
Rylin Enterprises

Copyright © 2012 by Randy G. Roy

Library and Archives Canada Cataloguing in Publication

Roy, Randy G.
        Heads Up ! / Randy G. Roy.

ISBN 978-0-9688462-4-7

        1. Horses--Training. 2. Horses--Grooming. 3. Horses--Judging.
4. Horsemanship. I. Title.

SF287.R68 2012   636.1'083   C2012-906771-7

First Published in 2012
by Rylin Enterprises

Printed in Canada
Porter Fine Printing Ltd.
Richmond Hill, Ontario

About the Cover
Designed by King Print. Illustration by Brenda Cuthbertson.

Dedication

Ian & Lynn

T HIS work is dedicated to all the people I have been so fortunate to work with over the years. There are too many names to list here, but it is their cumulative expertise and advise which enables me to write this book.

One special person must be mentioned in this dedication however, and that would be Lynn Millar.

Lynn and I go way back before she was married to Ian. We boarded our horses at the same barn – Lamoureaux's on Vanier Road in Aylmer, Quebec. I even remember her horses – The Rogue and Slow poke Mom. She was Lynn Doran then and we rode up Vanier Road to the Pink Road then to the Clock Road to Tic Toc Stables to show our horses. Probably five miles in all !!

Lynn was always about care, maintenance and stable management. Lynn was so passionate about all of these issues and god knows we discussed most all of them on our rides to and from the shows.

It is no wonder that she became the backbone of one of the most successful if not the most successful show operations in North America.

I so know that all of these tips are so dear to her heart and I find myself thinking of her with every Heads Up tip I write. I value all her knowledge and the quiet manner with which she conveyed it. I feel like she is such a big part of this book that she actually co-wrote it –

Thank You Lynn !!

Contents

Chapter VII

Preface

AS I go around barns and horseshows – whether it be mucking, grooming, teaching, training, course designing, judging and conducting clinics and seminars – I can't help but notice all of the things being done incorrectly. Sooooo – VOILA! Here it is: HEADS UP – my attempt at not only pointing out faux pas but to also offer solutions to better you and your horse in terms of safety and maintenance. I really hope by drawing your attention to these 153 don'ts or "whoa's", followed with corrective advise as "gallop" will assist you and your horse to a better now and future.

Introduction
by Dr. Helen Douglas

As one of the preeminent Hunter judges in North America, Randy Roy is a keen observer of horses and humans.

The idea for his latest book was born after many years of such observation in which Randy Roy noted that many small and large practices relating to the safety of both horse were being neglected. Perhaps, one might say, optimistically, that this was as a result of a systemic or individual lack of knowledge, rather than a casual disregard for safety. On the other hand, it could be surmised that it was a general laissez-faire, resulting from an "it couldn't happen to me" attitude that drove Randy Roy to the creation of this simple set of rules designed to prevent the majority of equine mishaps and maintenance errors.

Easy to read and understand, and equally easy to assimilate into your barn and show routine, these rules are well worth reading for both the novice and experienced horseman alike. For some, they may be a review, but for others starting into the sport, just reading one of these tips may help save the health, or even life, of a horse or its rider.

Mr. Roy has undoubtedly seen an accident or health problem related to disregard for each of the carefully thought out rules in his new book. Many of us admit to being less careful than we should towards our horses and in our own horse environments on a daily basis. Yet all of us have seen the hasty kick, the broken cross tie, the ill-fitting blanket and worse. Sometimes all we need is a kindly reminder to take care.

As a person who has had the responsibility for many beautiful horses, for evaluating top horse sport on a weekly basis and for imparting his wealth of knowledge with others, especially those keen to learn, through his articles and books, Randy has a genuine passion for the world of horses.

In his latest book, he is giving us that kindly reminder to take care.

Foreword
by Kim Kirton

Kim Kirton and Eric Lamaze

I am so excited about this book ! I am such a strong believer in stable management, safety and horse care.

It all started in Wellington, Florida when I had the pleasure of judging with Randy. We started to share with each other do's and don'ts regarding horsemanship and safety, which turned into a worldwide survey ! Then we thought, let's do a book and share these tips gathered from so many of the top judges, riders, trainers, vets, blacksmiths, barn managers and grooms.

I thank my father Gord Kirton, Rodney Jenkins and Wendy Waters for sharing these tips with me years ago, which I have followed and taught for 31 years. Heads Up !

Kim Kiton

Special Thanks

To William Stewart
For all his expert penmanship
and for making sense of me when I don't !

To Brenda Cuthbertson
For all of her amazing drawings and the sensational cover !

To Kim Kirton
For all her contributing tips !

To all my staff and clients
For all of their contributions !

To Dr. Helen Douglas
For all of her contributions !

Heads Up !

Chapter I
FROM THE BARN

1 – SUPERMAN

 Do not remove blankets by undoing the front of the blanket first.

 Always undo the leg straps and then the surcingles prior to undoing the front of the blanket. In the event your horse should bolt during this procedure, the blanket is then free to simply fall from the horse. Otherwise the blanket can slip back and entangle the rear legs – and I can assure you, he won't be happy about this.

2 – HANGING OUT

 Do not leave latches open on stall doors.

 When ever the horse leaves the stall be sure to close the latch as this commonly causes damage by snagging blankets on open latches or, even worse, catching the horses flesh.

3 – NETTED

 Never use hay nets in the stalls that are constructed of rope or nylon.

 A well secured hay bag with one opening will not sag while the hay is being removed (eaten) as a rope or nylon style hay net will. This excessive sagging can become a trap for your horse's legs.

4 – UNPINNED

 The use of bandage pins should never be permitted in securing leg bandages.

 I always recommend the use of a tape or Velcro (preferred) for this purpose. Horse can (and do) chew at their leg bandages so, I would rather the bandage fall away freely as it would with a tape or Velcro application as opposed to pins because the pins can easily cut the horse's lips, mouth and eyes or they can easily find their way into the horses foot or leg.

5 – Boo

 I think everyone knows this one… but I see it happen all the time! Never walk behind a horse without letting him know you are approaching him.

 A horse is quite capable of kicking out if he is startled, particularly if he doesn't see you coming first. When ever you are approaching a horse from behind, always be vocal to announce your approach and then gently touch him while continuing to speak. The element of surprise is something you *always* want to avoid.

6 – Demolition

 Do not secure cross-ties to the point that they cannot break.

 Your horse can find the cross-ties very restrictive and often will resist this, pulling back and becoming frantic. This situation can quickly accelerate to the point where the horse may fall to the ground. The use of binder-twine, with contact points between the hardware on the barn wall and at the end of the cross-tie, will ensure a breakage in the event the horse resists and pulls back.

7 – Bottoms Up

 Similarly, while in the stall the use of rope or tie-up material that will not break, and or rubber-ties with hooks is wrong.

 This is another case where your horse needs to be able to break his tie in the event he pulls back or gets his leg caught. The use of yarn or binder-twine between the contact points of the wall hardware and the rope-tie will ensure there is a necessary breakage when required. The use of rubber-ties with hooks is extremely hazardous as although the rubber can fail and break, the hook ends pose a very real danger of physical damage to your horse upon impact.

8 – ESCAPE

 When the horse is on the cross-ties do not secure the halter.

 On the cross-ties try to use a slip-halter or if you have to use a halter, make sure that you leave the lower strap un-fastened and secured on the same side – don't leave it hanging because it can swing and hit the horse in the eye. If for whatever reason the cross-ties don't give then when the horse pulls back and you have the halter unsecured or you are using a slip-halter – the halter will slip off the horse.

9 – UNDONE

 Putting a horse in a stall to dry off after bathing, with a scrim or sweat sheet that does not have a surcingle or straps to properly fasten is inviting disaster.

 Make sure that any blanket or cover you are using in the stall can be (and is) fastened and secured. The horse is most assuredly going to roll and without the cover being secured, it can easily wrap itself and get tangled around the horse leading to panic and injury.

10 – NAILED

WHAO Sweeping the aisle residue into the stalls after the Blacksmith has left is negligent.

GALLOP This can be done easily, particularly when there is new or inexperienced help in the barn. Instruct all barn personnel on the proper procedure of cleaning up after the Blacksmith has left by including that the residue be swept into a pile in the aisle and then disposed of into the garbage. This will avoid any unforeseen injuries occurring from nails being swept into the stalls or environment.

11 – DUSTING

 Sweeping the barn aisle before wetting or disinfecting it is a poor practice.

 Sweeping a dry floor in the barn not only raises the visible dust, but it can also spread harmful micro-organisms by making them airborne. In either case, there is a good chance of irritating eyes with particulate and of inhaling unwanted organisms. Make certain that a watercan filled with water and disinfectant is applied to the aisle floor before sweeping.

12 – LOUNGING

 If you must muck out your horse's stall with your horse in the stall, do not use a steel pronged fork.

 This scenario can easily lead to a stab wound. If you have no option to put it on the cross ties you can tie the horse into the corner until you are finished mucking out. Better yet, see if there is a plastic pronged fork to ensure there is no possible chance for injury. The plastic pronged forks are safer and lighter.

13 – MANURE ONLY

 It is un-wise to not have a strictly enforced smoking policy in any barn.

 With hay and shavings present in most barns you would think that smoking/smokers would be vigilant about this but I have seen many cases where there is negligence involving smoking in or around barns. This is such a careless act and the risks or dangers that it poses from potential fire can be catastrophic. There should be no smoking in the barn at anytime – without exceptions. No smoking within 50 feet of the barn is even better. Ensure that everyone checks that the cigarette butt is completely out and disposed of in container of water or sand. Signage in and around the barn banning smoking is strongly advised. Finally, make certain that everyone knows not to allow cigarette butts in the manure pile!

14 – OVERLOAD

**WHAO**   Watch out for over-blanketing.

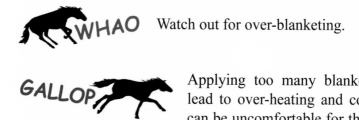**GALLOP** Applying too many blankets can lead to over-heating and colic. It can be uncomfortable for the horse and encourage rolling and the risk of getting cast. Monitor the weather, blanket accordingly and make sure you are not over-blanketing un-clipped horses in the winter.

15 – WRONG SIZE

 Do not try to squeeze your horse into a poorly fitted blanket.

 This can lead to blanket rubs and excessive rolling. The purpose of a blanket is for warmth and comfort. It is important that you always have a properly fitted and secure blanket for the horse's comfort.

16 – No Entry

When a horse is on the cross-ties never try to pass by with your horse by simply ducking under the cross-tie.

This practice (and it happens frequently!) is a disaster waiting to happen. The horse you are guiding under the cross-tie can easily lift his head and get caught by the cross-tie under his neck. This in turn, can pull the horse that is tied to the cross-ties. You can well imagine the events unfolding, with yourself smack in the middle of it! Always undo one cross-tie and gently push the tied horse to the wall he is tied to – allowing for lots of room for you and your horse to pass safely.

17 – RUNWAY

 Do not wear high-heels, flip-flops or other sandal type shoes while working around horses.

 Proper foot wear is required at all times when working around horses to protect you from being accidentally stepped on. This is a frequent and innocent occurrence and if you are not wearing appropriate foot wear you will feel it.

18 – WIRED

 **WHAO** Not un-plugging or turning off heating appliances after use in the barn.

 **GALLOP** Whether using space heaters or heaters designed to heat water in the barn, always ensure that they are turned off or better yet, un-plugged as this can easily lead to a fire. The horses have only you to rely on for their safety and well-being.

19 – NIGHTMARE

 Don't leave blankets on your horse ill-positioned or covered with shavings from the previous night.

 Always straighten and re-secure the blanket, brush off all the shavings. Without doing this the horse is often not comfortable and is unsightly and un-presentable.

20 – STUCK

 Turning your horse loose at the stall door while leading him into his stall is not a safe practice.

 You have no control in this scenario. Your horse could rush into his stall and you can be easily hurt during this. Additionally, if you lead him into the stall and turn him loose before turning him completely around and facing you, he can easily pin you to the wall. Many broken hands and dislocated shoulders are the result of this. Make certain that the stall door is wide open and then lead him in, turning him completely around to face you before removing the halter.

21

21 – CAUGHT

 It's not a good idea to ever use webbing or stall fronts that have large openings, or stall guards positioned too low.

 Large holes in the webbing can easily allow for the horses leg to get caught, and if the guard is positioned too low, it will be too inviting for the horse to try and get out, and then get caught. A single rubber guard positioned mid-way up the stall door opening or even a full flat rubber guard with no opening is adequate to prevent an attempted exit, and they are both safe.

22 – STRIKE ONE

 Standing in front of your horse or just under his head when you are twitching your horse is never a good idea.

 If you are positioned in this way while twitching, you are right within the striking zone when he strikes out or runs ahead. Always stand to the side of your horse when you are holding the twitch.

23 – BUZZ CUT

 Marching up to your horse with clippers in hand, turned on and buzzing away… is a sure-fire way to not getting the job done. This goes for the use of a vacuum cleaner as well, especially if these tools and sounds are all new to the horse. They can spook easily and set them right off!

 Instead, slowly approach them with the clippers turned off: Allowing them to see, smell and touch the clippers. You can then step back and turn the clippers on. Repeat the procedure with the clippers turned on.

24 – Spa

 **WHAO** Poor grooming habits can be corrected simply and easily.

 **GALLOP** People often use the curry comb and brush without a regular cleaning of these two utensils during the grooming process. They just continue with the same motions, working the dirt into the coat rather than out of the coat. Try to adopt a routine of tapping the curry comb on the back of the brush often and regularly during the currying process to clean the comb. Additionally, every so often you should clean the brush out by simply brushing against the curry comb. This only takes seconds but will make a huge difference in the appearance and hygiene of your horse. By the way, before you put the horse in his stall, the last thing you should do is get a damp sponge, lift the horse's tail and clean his bottom!

25 – REAR VIEW

Using double ended snaps when hanging feed and water buckets is great: Not paying attention to their positioning is not!

Always ensure that the opening mechanism of the double end snap is facing the wall, and not facing outward because it is too easy to catch your horse's eye or catch the blanket buckle or surcingle.

26 – Take-Out

 Don't leave full muck buckets or wheelbarrows in the aisle of the barn…. Ever!

 Everyone knows that manure attracts flies and the barn can become quickly over populated with flies unless the buckets are removed as soon as they are full and at the end of each day. Frequent trips to the manure pile will help keep the flies away!

27 – HOUDINI

 Leaving the barn for the evening using only the stall guards as opposed to the stall doors to secure your horses is a mistake.

 It's not a question of whether or not a horse can escape in is this situation as he most certainly will. Always secure the stall doors with the latches closed before leaving for the evening. When you are at the shows, put the extra effort into securing the stall door with a rope to be certain and for peace of mind.

28 – WHOOPS, WRONG BRUSH

 Never comb out a horses tail with a comb or a harsh/ stiff brush.

 Before attempting to brush the tail always apply Show Sheen first, then use a soft brush or separate the tail hair with your fingers. The tail hair can become quite brittle and prone to breakage so, using a dressing prior to brushing will lubricate and protect the hair from damage.

29 – OFF-COURSE

 Never use a wheelbarrow to block a stall door when mucking out with the horse loose in the stall.

 An open stall door is an invitation for a loose horse to exit the stall. The wheelbarrow is not recognized by your horse as a deterrent but it is enough of a menace to cause damage and injury if the horse does decide to exit. Secure the horse with a breakaway tie to the wall or use the cross ties, or put him in another stall while you are mucking out.

30 – AMUSEMENT PARK

 Do not install foreign objects such as toys, balls or other boredom beaters in the horse's stall using chains or snaps as they can be hazardous.

 Always seek out the approval of the barn manager and allow him to secure the selected object safely in the stall.

31 – TENDONS IN

When bandaging or putting on Polos never pull wraps toward you. Never use an elastic product such as Vet-Wrap as a stable bandage. Pulling the straps toward you pulls the tendons outward, which is not the natural positioning for the tendons.

GALLOP

When bandaging always think "tendons – in", pushing the wraps away from you. Try to start low enough so that you have enough at the top to cover the whole wrap or leg area. It is important to apply constant and even pressure so that there is equal support from bottom to top. Secondly, if you have to use Vet-Wrap or elastic products, always ensure you have adequate padding to prevent tendon swelling and even bowed tendons.

32 – NAME THAT HORSE

 Do not leave your horse in a stall at the show or at home without a sign notifying passersby of his show name and barn name.

 Ensure that both his barn and show name are on the stall door at the show and at the barn so that the Vet, Groom, Farrier, Shipper, Braider etc. can identify the proper horse to handle.

33 – OUT OF REACH

 Providing your horse with treats too frequently can create problematic behavior.

 Timing is everything. Some people give treats before entering the ring or after leaving the ring as encouragement. Others simply provide treats regularly throughout the day. This creates expectation and your horse will quickly begin looking for his treat, being persistent in nipping, biting and climbing all over you personally. In short, your horse will be spoiled. If you want to give your horse treats for a job well done you can put them in the feed bucket as a surprise. This will avoid nuisance behavior and the grooms will appreciate it as they will not have to deal with an obnoxious horse.

34 – Today's Orders

 Not providing clear communication relating to the daily status of your stalled horse is negligent.

 An erasable board (chalk board or grease board) on the stall door is perfect for this. Anyone handling your horse (including yourself) can up-date daily instructions as required: Name, wet hay, types of boots for turnout, stall rest, water off, bath day, vet or farrier today etc.

35 – DAY OFF

 Not having a shared work list or chart posted in your barn can lead to confusion and mishaps.

 This is essential to have in every barn. Each horse in your barn will have different requirements and usually these requirements will change daily so a work chart or daily/weekly planner should be posted in the barn for everyone to review regularly. This chart will identify each horse by name and includes instructions by day pertaining to each horse for up to one full week. We use short symbols to describe detailed requirements, appointments or events and we have a symbol key at the margin of the chart for reference. To review a sample of this work chart please refer to the back of chapter seven.

36 – RUNNING THE GAUNTLET

 Do not leave shovels, forks, rakes or brooms loose in the aisles or grooming stalls.

 Loose tools or utensils can be hazardous to both you and your horse as well as being unsightly. Always hang the working items on wall hooks or in the feed room or junk stall when not in use. Please ensure that all forks and rakes are cleaned off prior to storage.

37 – Class Act

 Not taking adequate precautions involving horses that roll a lot can lead to panic and injury. A horse that tends to frequently roll in his stall can become stuck in awkward and dangerous positions.

 Banking up the stall walls will help in preventing your horse from getting cast. I recommend putting an anti-cast roller on him with a blanket underneath so that it will prevent him from rolling over and the blanket will prevent a sore back.

38 – 6' 2"

**WHAO** Never directly approach your horse or pony with a measuring stick without allowing them to inspect it first, or what you were hoping was to be 14 hands has suddenly become 15 hands!

**GALLOP** Most horses and ponies will be alarmed by a sudden appearance of a measuring stick, standing taller and potentially disqualifying them due to height regulations. Quietly approach your horse or pony and let them get familiar with the measuring stick before opening it up. Make your movements slow as to not surprise them. As a last resort you can cover the eye on the side you are measuring. It is a good idea to get the horse accustomed to the measuring stick at home prior to a show so that he is relaxed about and you can get an accurate measure.

39 – WINNER

 When using leg straps don't just wrap around each leg without criss-crossing the strap before securing.

 In the stall, paddock or van, the straps need to be criss-crossed to avoid slipping of the blanket. This also helps to avoid chaffing and irritation of the hind legs.

40 – LOCK AND KEY

 Improper storage of medication, syringes, needles and other supplies is just asking for trouble.

 All equipment, medical utensils and medication should be stored away, securely locked and out of site. This is important because random access to these supplies can result in incorrect administration, damage and even theft. The possession of medications and equipment is a large and expensive responsibility so, please ensure that you have a strict barn policy as it relates to the storage and handling of this material.

Heads Up !

Chapter II
FROM HOME

41 – TECHNOLOGY VS. RIDING

 Do not ride with a communications device or a cell phone on your person.

 Always leave your device (this includes Pagers) in the barn or better yet, in your vehicle. Riding is not unlike driving your car: It requires all of your attention and faculties. Additionally, an unexpected ring, alarm or a full symphony orchestra rendition of the William Tell Overture - signaling an in-coming call can easily startle your horse.

44

42 – GIRTHY

 Not checking that your girth is tight before mounting.

 Always check for a correctly fitted Girth prior to mounting. A Girth fitted too tightly will irritate your horse and could lead to a difficult ride. A loosely fitted Girth increases your risk of slippage, and losing your mount rather abruptly. The Girth needs to be just snug enough as to not slide.

43 – Skipping

 Do not jump in Draw Reins that are too loose.

 Jumping in Draw Reins that are too loose can easily cause a mishap by catching the rider's foot or catching the horse's leg in them. Always attach the Draw Reins or use a Yoke if you have to use Draw Reins. I don't like to see them used in jumping at all because they are too artificial.

44 – Stunt Riding

 Never attempt a mounted stirrup adjustment with your leg up and across the saddle.

 Always adjust a stirrup (if you are mounted) with your foot in the stirrup. This can prevent a potentially disastrous injury if the horse decides to bolt.

45 – TRAPPED

 A dangerous combination – Your horse is wearing a full-cheek bit while wearing shin boots.

 This is an accident just waiting to happen. The horse can easily drop his head to scratch and get the shin boot caught in the full-cheek bit, trapping his leg and head... over he goes! Polo wraps or boots without straps can help to prevent this while the horse is wearing the full-cheek snaffle or even better, wearing no boots at all will avoid this incident entirely.

46 – LONG GONE

 When turning your horse out don't just open the gate and let him go.

 While standing at the gate, always turn the horse to face you before letting him go. This will avoid a possible injury to your self as he may kick upon being released – from the excitement of freedom. Additionally, always ensure that the gate is closed behind you before you release the horse: If the gate is left open upon his release there is a very good chance he will bolt straight back to the barn.

47 – GONE FLYING

 Leading a horse by the halter or in a slip-grooming halter alone is un-wise.

 Always check that the halter is completely fastened and always lead with a shank attached as the horse can spook easily and then he will be loose without a shank.

48 – Cooking

 Do not use boots that are un-lined or have rubber exposed on the inside of the boot.

 We always use boots that are lined with felt or sheepskin or Polos. Boots that are not lined or have exposed rubber will cause sweating which in turn can cause irritation and even blistering.

49 – No Give

 Never allow your horse to be turned out wearing a nylon halter.

 Nylon will not break. When your horse decides to roll he can easily get his leg caught and this could lead to a very serious injury. Insist on having your horse turned out wearing either a leather halter which will break, or have him turned out with no halter at all.

50 – ALL TIED UP

 Putting hay rolls in the fields with binder twine still attached needs to be avoided.

 Ensure that all hay rolls have had the binder twine cut and removed, or put the hay rolls into a secured hay enclosure.

51 – RAILS ONLY

 Do not leave jump cups or standards without rails as horses can cut or injure themselves.

 Always turn the standard away to the side or remove the pin and cup, putting the pin into the cup at a lower level. Do not leave the pin or cup on the ground where a horse can step on them.

52 – UNDERCOVER

 Using turn-out blankets that do not have leg straps should not be allowed.

 Horses always roll when they are turned out and if the blanket is not secured it will move in all directions during this procedure, causing panic. Always ensure that you use blankets for turn-out that have leg straps and make sure they are fastened and then cross them so that they will not rub and irritate the horse.

53 – DON'T GO THERE

 Riding or guiding your horse through unsecured or too narrow an opening.

 Make sure that all swinging doors are secured and all stall doors are completely opened before leading your horse through. Don't even attempt to ride or guide your horse through an opening you are questioning because it is too easy for you to get dislodged or catch the horse's hip.

54 – PLOUGHED

 Do not leave harrows laying down in the ring or paddocks.

 Horses can easily get caught up in a harrow. We always ensure that the harrows are completely removed from the ring or paddock after use and placed leaning against a fence or a wall – where they can be seen.

55 – STITCH IN TIME

 Don't forget to periodically inspect the stitching of your tack.

 A Girth, Bridle, Martingale, Breast Plate or Saddle is only as good as its stitching is. The stitching is your security and a failure in the stitching can prove to be disastrous. Be sure to go over your tack now and then, and if there is anything that appears doubtful have it re-stitched or if need be, have it replaced.

56 – HOME ALONE

 Riding or jumping alone without anyone else knowing you are riding are alone is a mistake.

 Always try to ride with a partner so that in the event of a mishap, there is someone there to assist you. At the very least, you should advise the groom or the manager that you are riding so they can periodically check on you.

57 – OFF LIMITS

 Never attempt to clip your horse's eyelashes.

 No trimming of eyelashes ever! Horses spend a lot of time in the dark and they use their eyelashes to feel their way around, much like a cat uses its whiskers to gently sense objects around it. A horses eyelashes are their light… and they look good too!

58 – Do-Do Road

 Do not leave manure to build up in your paddocks.

 Aside from being unhealthy and unsanitary, this is also unsightly. It leaves everyone with the impression that your horse is not cared for and it speaks poorly of the barn management. Be sure to remove all manure and or have the paddock harrowed.

59 – ALL IN THE WASH

 Stop! Read those labels on the laundry detergent container before doing your horse's laundry.

 There are so many detergent products on the market and many of them contain dyes and perfumes that can be harmful to your horse. Some of these components can create great irritation, rashes and even allergic reactions. Always check the label to ensure the detergent is free of these ingredients and if in doubt, ask someone knowledgeable whether or not the detergent you have selected is a good choice.

60 – Twos Company

When you are turning two horses out together it is a mistake to bring them out or bring them back in separately.

All too frequently the horse left behind will become excited and could get hurt. In a situation like this you should ensure that there are two people leading each of the turn outs at the same time and two people bringing them back at the same time as well. This should help to avoid any unnecessary mishaps.

61 – HEAD FIRST

 When bathing a horse, the head is most often overlooked because it can be a difficult task. The horse's head is viewed most often however and for this reason, skipping the head-washing is a mistake.

 The following tips can ensure an easier head-washing process: Firstly, get a step ladder so that you are at eye level with your horse. Secondly, with a soft wetted sponge you can gently massage the head all over and then begin the rinse. Thirdly, correct rinsing involves repeated trips up and down the ladder with a sponge soaked with clean, clear water and gently squeezed over the horses head. DO NOT HOSE THE HORSES HEAD – the horse will back away as this process can hurt them if the spray is too strong. Gently squeezing a soaked sponge over their head will eventually lead to their acceptance of water on their head and can lead to the eventual acceptance of a weak spray from a hose.

62 – BRONCO

 If your horse is sensitive to the girth you need to pay attention, particularly while mounting.

 After fastening the saddle strap sufficiently enough as to not slip (but not too snug), walk the horse around until he becomes accustomed to the fit and seems comfortable. This is important to do prior to an attempted mounting because he can react negatively during the mount and this can lead to bucking or injury.

63 – Posé

 Unsupervised dogs around horses are never a good idea.

 Even well trained dogs can become over stimulated when horses are being exercised or are turned out and they begin to act up. Dogs running loose in the barn can easily spook a horse, especially if the dog goes underneath the horse. Try to ask everyone to keep their dogs on a leash, in their vehicle with the window down if the weather permits or better yet, leave their dog at home.

64 – HALF HOOKED

 When leading a horse that is tacked up do not leave the stirrups down. This practice can lead to the stirrups being caught on anything in the immediate vicinity.

 Always run the stirrups up and put the leathers through properly before leading your horse anywhere.

65 – WHAT JUMP

Not planning or carrying out regular ring and footing maintenance can cause lameness and permanent damage to your footing.

Do not repeatedly harrow around the jumps without moving them. This happens often and the problem with this is the deepest ruts develop just in front of the jump and at the landing side. In a busy ring you may not have regular access to these areas to repair the ruts. At least once or twice a week you need to move all of the jumps to the side and harrow the area where the jumps were stationed. You will notice that these areas have the highest elevation.

66 – Squeaky Clean

 Insufficient rinsing after a soap bath is more of a problem than you may understand.

 A horse's skin is twelve times more sensitive than human skin so removing soap residue is more important than many people realize. Without full removal of soap the skin can quickly become irritatingly dry and itchy. It also leads to a dull coat. After a soap bath take your scraper and scrape off all of the soap before rinsing with clear water. This ensures complete removal of the soap and it is faster than having to repeat the rinse to get all of the soap out. Adding vinegar to the rinse water enhances soap removal and the bonus is that vinegar acts as a fly repellant!

67 – FREE SHANK

 Never attempt to keep a gate closed by simply tying off a shank.

 Horses are escape artists! It doesn't take long for a horse to figure out how to untie the loops of a tied off shank and take off. They will play with the tied shank until it gives way. Always use a proper latch or chain and snap to secure the gate closed.

68 – PONY RIDES

 Doing ring work and circling all the time and never taking your horse for hacks is not good for your horse.

 Do some of your fitness work at the walk and trot in fields and on roads and don't forget that hacking is very important for your horse's mind.

69 – ALL WALK PLEASE

At home and in schooling don't just go into the ring and immediately begin trotting or cantering.

Try walking for at least 5 or 10 minutes to loosen up stiff joints from the stall confinement. This makes for a pleasant and relaxed start.

70 – COOLING OFF

 Going immediately to the wash rack or stall with a sweaty, hard breathing horse from a hard work out.

 This can easily promote colic in your horse. Always ensure that you walk long enough after a work out to allow the horse's breathing to return to a normal and relaxed state before taking him to the wash rack or his stall.

71 – Towed

 Do not wrap the lead shank around your hand or wrist as you can easily end up in tow behind a runaway horse.

 Hold the shank with both hands securely. If the horse bolts or rears or runs in any direction you have both hands to control him. If you lose your grip with one hand, you have the other one in contact with the shank to control him.

Chapter III
FROM THE SHOW

72 – IN TOW

 Never attempt to lunge any horse while it is wearing only a halter.

 Always use a bridle while lunging as this ensures your control during the exercise.

73 – Loose-End

 Do not allow leading or grazing on the end of a lead-shank that is too long.

 Proximity to your horse is critical when leading and you need to ensure that the lead-shank is shortened up because with excessive space between you and the horse there is always a risk of the horse turning and kicking you.

74 – SMILE

Do not hang tack hooks in the grooming stalls.

Always hang the tack hook away from the grooming stall, out of reach from the horse as they can get caught on the hook quite easily.

75 – Highbeams

 Do not put your horse away with ear plugs in his ears. This is so easy to do on busy days!

 Always check for ear plugs prior to putting your horse away. We have a check list for anyone who is responsible for night-check and looking for any remaining ear plugs is on this list! Sound silly… but it can happen.

76 – Under-Wraps

 Not checking for proper fit when applying bandages can lead to problems.

 When bandages are fitted too loosely the horse will try and kick them off, and if they are fitted too tightly this can lead to a bowed tendon and can be uncomfortable. Wraps or bandages should be applied snuggly, with enough cushion to provide support and to be comfortable.

77 – OVER STUFFED

 The use of a saddle pad that is too small or a poorly positioned saddle pad is a bad scenario.

 The saddle pad is designed to protect the horse from direct contact with the leather of the saddle. If the saddle pad is too small or if it is positioned incorrectly the saddle will rub and create irritation. Always check that the saddle pad is large enough to ensure there is no direct contact, that it is covering the wither and not positioned behind the wither, and that both sides are even – with no bunching of the pad.

78 – WHIPS

 The use of stirrup leathers that are too long can create some unforeseen problems.

 When stirrup leathers are too long (this happens frequently with ponies) they can act as little whips on the sides of the horse or pony. Purchase stirrup leathers that are properly fitted or cut the ones you have to the appropriate length, and please ensure that there is not too much left remaining.

79 – DRIVING

 Riding with reins that are too long and hanging down by the shoulder is sloppy and dangerous.

 This situation can lead to a foot or leg getting caught, and the irritation it can cause by continuous slapping against the shoulder of the horse is not necessary. Firstly, try to purchase the correct length of rein. Secondly, you can always take the rein to a tack shop and have them shortened/adjusted to the correct length. Please do not simply tie a knot to shorten the length of rein as this appears tasteless.

80 – UNHARNESSED

 Riders should never mount or jog back to the ring with their chin strap undone.

 Always ensure that the riders have their chin strap fastened while around any horse or pony. A fall or a kick can lead to serious head injuries if the helmet falls off.

81 – No Room

 Not providing enough space between yourself and the rider in front of you while jogging back into the ring.

 It is important that you continually watch the rider ahead of you and that you make sure that rider is well ahead of you before you begin to jog (with your chin strap fastened). This is a situation where it is too easy to close in on the rider in front of you quickly, risking a kick or a collision.

82 – LAWRENCE OF ARABIA

 Do not ride with your jacket or top un-done.

 Before moving or riding off check to make sure your top or jacket is zipped or buttoned properly because if it flies open during your ride it can easily spook your horse and off you go!

83 – D-BITTED

 Do not ever cross tie directly to the bit.

 In the event your horse should pull back and want to break loose, a direct cross tie to the bit can create serious damage and injury to your horse. Put a halter over the bridle then cross tie to the halter or remove the bridle altogether.

84 – Run-away Prize

 During presentation such as Classics or Derbies, do not accept awards while you are mounted.

 Having a large bouquet of flowers or a trophy thrust at the horse can easily spook him, and with your arms full you won't be in a position to stop him from performing a solo victory gallop!   Instead, have the presenter hold the flowers or trophy until you return from the victory gallop and have dismounted.

85 – Spit The Bit

Do not let the bit hang too low in the horse's mouth.

It is important that you raise the bit so that it rests close to the first molar tooth and that there is no room for the tongue to move up and over the bit.

86 – JAWS

Do not allow nosebands to be so loose as to permit the horse to open his mouth, resisting the contact and getting strong.

Always tighten the noseband right up and if you can't, then make another hole in the noseband to ensure that it is snug. This is a sure way to regain control and reduce resistance from your horse.

87 – Hɪ-Lᴏᴡ

 Do not show or jump with an improperly fitted Standing Martingale.

 Take the time to do up the Martingale so that it is at a comfortable length. If the length is too long the Martingale loses its functionality and your horse's head will go too high. When a Martingale's length is too short it will appear restricting and stiff, and this can influence the jump.

88 – NO PASSING

 If a horse is running loose and galloping toward you, do not stand in front of him to stop him.

 This may sound basic but some people are not aware that a horse will not stop because you are standing in front of him when he is running loose or galloping – He will run you over. Always wave your arms while stepping to the side for your safety.

89 – PROTECTION

 Do not attempt to lunge without a whip or without wearing gloves.

 The whip keeps the horse at a distance and moving while the glove can protect you from a severe friction burn should the horse decide to bolt. This usually happens only once to a person – but it doesn't have to happen at all.

90 – Wardrobe

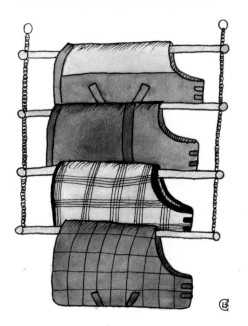

 Don't hand-walk or turnout your horses in their stable blankets.

 This will create prominent and unattractive shoulder rubs. Remove the stable blankets before turnout and replace with the appropriate blanket. Hand walk in a secured, light sheet.

91 – INSPECTOR

 Never put a horse immediately into a stall at a show without first inspecting the stall thoroughly for nails or other sharp objects.

 Go first through the stalls and check for any of these kinds of objects that could cause injury. You can easily do this while you are preparing to bed them, putting up buckets etc. before letting the horse into the stall for the night.

92 – ESCAPE ROUTE

 Never attempt to remove blankets or wraps while the stall door is open.

 Your horse will try to escape if the door is left open. Put up a webbing or close the door completely before unwrapping or attempting to re-wardrobe your horse.

#93 – Wrong Turnout

 Not providing your groom with a check list while at the show.

 Don't assume that your groom is aware of all of the regulations involved in showing. Provide your groom with a check list so that he can ensure that your horse is prepared when standing at the gate and ready to jog back into the ring. A tail wrap left on or even a simple change of Bridle will result in your elimination. The check list should include the removal of all wraps, blankets or scrim.

94 – PERM

 Do not bandage legs that are wet or damp.

 Moisture on the legs prior to bandaging will wrinkle and curl the hair, create bandage rubs, and will not provide the support you are looking for from a properly dried and braced leg. It is important to ensure that the leg is thoroughly dried before bandaging. You can take the horse out to graze while allowing the legs to dry or you can towel dry before applying the brace and then the bandages.

95 – Douche

 Unbraiding your horse while the hair is dry is not recommended.

 Unbraiding a dry forelock, mane or especially tails is guaranteeing some damage. The hair is too delicate in this state, being tightly bound and dry at the same time: Working the hair out of a weave in this way will break the hair. You should completely saturate the forelock, mane or tail with water before beginning the process of unbraiding. This will allow for a much faster unbraiding and will protect the hair from unnecessary damage and loss.

96 – Lame

 Braiding your horse while standing on concrete floors is something I discourage.

 A lot of braiders will braid a horse with the horse standing on concrete for long periods of time. This can make the horse very stiff and possibly foot sore. Ask your braider to braid the horse in the familiarity and comfort of their stall, on a nice soft cushion of bedding.

97 – Horses Only

 **WHAO**   Don't stand in front of or behind the jump in the schooling area.

 **GALLOP**   Standing in these locations can be unsafe for you because the horse can quickly knock a standard into you if you are located behind the jump. A quick run out can flatten you if you are in front of the jump. The best place to stand is on the side and far enough away from the standards so they cannot reach you in the event of a mishap.

98 – Nailed & Screwed

 Do not work with your horse in an area with U nails or screw eyes that are not adequately screwed into the wall.

 Inadequately installed U nails or screw eyes can be bumped with some impact from a horse and the possibility of injury from stepping on one is too great to your horse. Ensure that all U nails or screw eyes are fully screwed into the wall with your screwdriver so there is no chance of loosening and falling to the floor.

99 – STAIRWAY TO ?

 Don't leave an unattended horse in the grooming stall with unsecured items such as ladders, bags or forks.

 Ensure that all items are removed or secured to the wall before leaving the stall even if it's for a few minutes. The horse will definitely find a way to become entangled and this could lead to possible injuries.

100 – WHICH WAY DO I GO

Relying only on your trainer to know the jumping course without knowing it yourself is irresponsible and almost always leads to poor results.

Someone once said "failing to plan is like planning to fail". Always and without exception, study the course and memorize the sequence or the numbers of the jumps in the Horsemanship Classes so, when you are called back in the ring for the Ride-Offs you will know the correct jumps. There is nothing wrong with double and even triple checking the numbers on the jumps because in the end, you are the only one responsible for getting it correct!

101 – TUNNEL VISION

 Lunging horses in a small circle can create problems.

 Make certain that you are lunging in a large enough circle to avoid damaging the hocks and joints. Where ever possible try to tie two lunge lines together, ensuring they are covering a sufficiently large area. Remember the whip to keep them extended on the lunge line and moving!

102 – HOPSCOTCH

 Walking and grazing with a chain shank doubled back in a loop is a mistake.

 The chance of your horse placing his foot through the looped end of the shank is very high and this can lead to big trouble. Put the shank over his nose or fasten the end snap of the shank directly to the halter with no loop.

103 – No Gift

 If you know your horse is a kicker, don't ride around where there are other horses or at the Ingate without giving other riders a heads-up.

 A good idea is to tie a red ribbon to your horses tail – drawing attention to your horse in this way will make people aware of the situation so they can take the necessary precautions.

104 – 911

  Leaving your horse in his stall for the night at a show without providing a contact name and phone number is neglectful.

Always post on a billboard or chalkboard the names and contact information of more than one person in the event of an emergency. The Groom or the Rider's information is a good example.

105 – Brand New

 Attempting to show with a new saddle or new tack is wrong for a number of reasons.

 Firstly, a new saddle's leather is not supple enough to ensure security. It can loosen a rider easily. Likewise, new tack will not move sufficiently (think flexibility) as well as "broken-in" tack. It's also not comfortable for the horse. Secondly, a new saddle and tack can be distracting when being viewed in a show by a Judge and it leaves the impression that the rider is somewhat of a novice. Take the time to stain and oil your tack repeatedly until it darkens sufficiently before you use it at the show level.

106 – REVERSE

 Leading a horse while you are seated in a mobile vehicle such as a golf-cart, pick-up truck, bicycle or motor-bike is an all too common practice and should be avoided. This is an extremely dangerous method of leading your horse because it can easily (and quickly) lead to serious injury to both you and your horse.

 Always lead your horse while you are on foot. I know that some of the distances to cover at shows can be considerable but this is the safest way to lead for you, your horse, other horses and for other people as well. And it is healthy!

107 – No Parking

 Going into the schooling area to set jumps with your horse in tow is asking for trouble.

 This is another common practice that needs to be checked. Anyone bringing their horse into the ring while they are attempting to set jumps is endangering everyone in the immediate vicinity. You don't have control of your horse when your hands are being used to set the jumps and your attention is divided between the two tasks of controlling your horse and setting jumps. The horse is in your way when you are setting the jumps and there are others that are jumping near-by, which can startle your horse… there are simply too many things that can go very wrong in this scenario. Please get someone to hold your horse outside of the ring if you have to enter the ring to set jumps.

108 – Bon Apétit

 Clients who turn up at the show in the early morning and immediately ride off with their horse without greeting or acknowledging the Trainer or the Groom is a display of poor etiquette.

 Try to remember that the Trainer and the Groom are often on site hours before your arrival. A cordial greeting and perhaps offering them a coffee and/or a muffin is a pleasant and very much appreciated way of starting the long day off well. It's all about attitude and everyone wants to have a good day.

109 – To All Good Men

 Trainers or managers who leave a show at the end of the day without acknowledging the grooms in some positive way sends a negative message.

 This is all too common. Regardless of whether the show performance was successful or not, the grooms have worked a long and arduous day and they deserve to be recognized for doing their job well. Grooms that know they are valued will maintain their motivation and perform well consistently, day in and day out.

110 – Plugged In

 Using a fan in your horse's stall needs to be thought out prior to installation.

 You need to make certain that the placement of the fan is such that the horse cannot reach it; particularly the cord, where chewing of the cord could have *shocking* results (sorry…. couldn't resist).

111 – GARBAGE ONLY

 Lunging without considering others in close proximity is unsafe and offensive.

 Please remember that your specific lunging practices may be effective for your horse – such as excessive cracking of the whip or shaking a noisy bag at the end of a stick, but these same actions can spook the other horses. This situation can quickly lead to injuries. Keep the whip cracking down or to a minimum and save the bag for the garbage!

112 – NO SCHOOLING

 When going into the schooling area to set jumps all that is required is yourself.

 Leave grooming boxes, rain gear, coolers, dogs and horses at the in-gate area. There is not enough room in the schooling area and this added clutter is hazardous.

113 – HOMEWORK

 Not being aware of the distances between the jumps and how this relates to the required strides can trip you up!

 It is your job to know this. Always study the number feet between the jumps and the number of strides required between the jumps so that you can execute this as required. Remember, a Judge in an Equitation class may ask you how many strides say, in a line of 72 feet…. You need to have the answer.

114 – SCISSOR HAPPY

 When cutting the bailer twine off of the bales of hay with a knife or scissors do not stab them into the bale afterwards as they will most assuredly be served to a horse with the next meal.

 It is a good idea to have some twine attached to the scissors or knife for easy hanging on a hook in the feed room, stall or near the hay pile or wagon.

115 – Freedom Rings

 Don't spend the majority of your show day socializing. Remember that your horse is locked up.

 I have included this tip because I see this all too often at the shows. Take the time throughout the day as often as possible to remove your horse from the stall, to walk, stretch and graze… when he is happier he may even show better.

116 – Two, Three, Fours A Crowd

 Bandaging: Don't allow someone to help you. The same person should bandage all of the legs.

 You need to bandage all four legs yourself, to ensure an even constant pressure because another person will not apply the same pressure as you are applying, and it is important that all four legs are equally supported. When you bandage an injured leg you MUST bandage the opposite leg because the horse will displace his weight to the uninjured leg and this will require sufficient support as well.

117 – Unwrapped

 Bandaging your horse while out in the open or tied outside to a trailer.

 Your horse needs to be confined to a stall with cross ties or a grooming stall when being bandaged. The horse needs to see that he is confined and cannot simply move away or run off. Sudden movements or attempts at these kinds of movements are greatly reduced when in an enclosed area. Bandaging outside without some kind of confinement can lead to serious injury to the person bandaging.

118 – OUT OR IN

When setting jumps at home or in the schooling area pay attention to how you secure the rail after adjusting for height.

Don't just barely place the pin in the cup or place it only half way through the cup. This looks sloppy and will not secure the rail, allowing it to fall too easily. Always put the pin all the way through the cup and make certain it can be seen coming through the other side.

119 – SHOW TIME

 Not preparing and planning well enough for a show can prove disastrous.

 Failing to plan is like planning to fail. Just ask any of my staff about my famous lists! At the show we stay organized by building a show chart and posting it so that everyone involved has access to it. This is a well planned schedule that includes everyone's names and duties, times, horses names etc. This is a useful tool that ensures everything runs smoothly while attending the show.

120 – DOUBLE HEADER

 Never tie your horse to the pipes, hoses or any similar fixtures at the show's wash rack.

 This is an accident waiting to happen. When you are washing your horse at a show you should hold him with one of your hands while washing, or ground tie the horse. Another possibility is to ask a friend to hold your horse so that you can use both hands for bathing and have a chat at the same time.

#121 – DOUBLE DUTCH

Not maintaining control from beginning to end of lunging can create a dangerous entanglement for both you and your horse.

I have witnessed people chasing the horse out to the end of the lunge line immediately upon entering the ring. The next time they lunge this horse he will surely bolt with the person in tow. I have also seen people allow the horse to turn and come toward them while lunging as well as allowing the horse to turn and go in the other direction on their own. These mistakes allow for a serious, tangled and dangerous mess. When you arrive in the lunging area, make sure you are wearing gloves and that you are holding a lunge whip. Be sure the horse has a bridle on and begin to let the lunge line out gradually, unraveling in an orderly fashion as the horse takes on the distance you allow using the lunge whip.

122 – LAST HORSE STANDING

 If your horse is a reluctant jogger never smack, wave a towel or hit him with a crop to encourage the jog.

 This is a sure fire way to get kicked at the ingate and an unsuspecting assistant or anyone in close proximity will be on the receiving end of that kick. Instead, go into the schooling area and practice jogging by making a clucking sound as you ask the horse to begin a jog. Have someone help you from a safe distance by clucking and eventually he will respond and follow you.

Chapter IV
From The Van

123 – TOO TIGHT

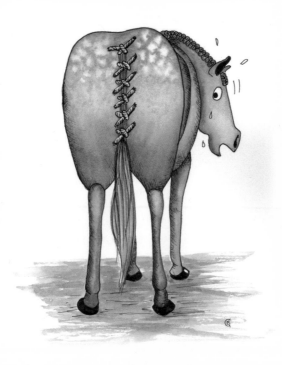

 Shipping with tail wraps on or putting on wraps that are too tight for extended periods of time is problematic.

 If you know your horse has a tendency to rub, then ship him facing backward. Ensure that you have left instructions with your braider not to wrap too tightly, and to never wet the wrap because as it dries it will shrink and tighten.

124 – Snug

 Shipping horses in a simple leather halter may seem innocent but it leads to problems.

 Shipping in a simple leather halter can cause loss of hair and unsightly rub marks as the horse will lean on the tie ups on long trips. Always plan to ship using a shipping halter lined with sheepskin or purchase the package of sheepskin liner that has Velcro so that you can remove it and wash later.

125 – Party Time

 Shipping halters that are not properly secured before shipping.

 Always ensure that the strap is all the way through the buckle as you would the buckle of your pants. If there is even a chance that the halter can come off, it will. The horse will rub against the trailer wall and the halter will slip off easily. A lose horse in the van is not a good thing!

126 – WATER SLIDE

Do not use loading ramps that are rubber covered and possibly wet without covering with a coco mat before loading or unloading your horses.

A length of coco mat that can cover the ramps is easily rolled up and stored in the van. It takes only seconds to roll the coco mat out and it will provide a slip-free surface for your horse. A slip or a fall during loading will not help a reluctant loader and can be dangerous for a fast un-loader.

127 – LONG RIDE

 Putting your horse directly into his stall after a long van ride is asking for trouble.

 You need to walk the horse for at least 5 minutes prior to placing him into the stall. This will loosen up the stiff joints after standing for so many hours in the van. It will allow the horse to become familiar with his surroundings and relax. Once the horse is in his stall, take his temperature after 30 minutes to make sure all is normal. A bran mash is recommended to ensure he is hydrated and his digestion and bowel movements are normal.

128 – Not Today

WHAO Do not attempt to do too much with your horse after a long haul.

GALLOP After a long trip your horse may seem ready and excited but he is not completely recovered. For three days the horse can walk, graze, turnout and have a light workout. Take his temperature regularly and making sure he is eating and drinking well. Putting your horse to work too early after a long haul can quickly and adversely impact your horse's health and well being.

129 – LONG HAUL

Don't plan a long haul in a trailer without preparing your horse physically well ahead of time.

If a horse is unfit or has poor muscle tone prior to a long haul, always ensure he either goes into the trailer's box stall or if not, prepare him by building up his muscle tone through exercise well before the planned trip. These trips can be physically demanding, stressful and exhausting. An unconditioned horse can experience shipping fever and possible colic from these trips. It is good idea to provide an oil and bran mash before leaving and ensure that there is water and hay available to the horse constantly.

130 – First Class

Leaving for a long haul with your horse without consulting your check list can lead to a very unpleasant trip.

Check list for long hauls:
- Shipping halter is secured
- Breakable tie that is long enough to reach water and hay
- Short enough tie to ensure no chewing on the neighbor
- Hay bag or hay net is full
- Accessible water
- Bedding to encourage urination
- Sufficient ventilation
- Blankets are secure
- Wraps are secure enough to prevent slipping
- Spare halter

131 – Slow & Steady

 When self shipping horses, you cannot drive as you normally do in your personal vehicle.

 When you are transporting horses in a van attached to your truck, try to imagine you have a bucket of water behind you that you cannot spill or tip over. Accelerate, brake and execute all turns slowly and with caution, as you have a valued cargo. Mishaps can easily turn your horse into a "bad shipper" and he will refuse to load the next time you attempt to get him into a van.

Chapter V
From The Farrier

132 – DaVinci

WHAO   Applying hoof oil too frequently is a common error.

GALLOP   Try to limit the amount of hoof oil you use and apply it only once, when it will count the most – as in at the in-gate before showing. Applying hoof oil before going into the ring, then before the jog and then again before the under saddle is too much hoof oil altogether and will make the foot too soft.

133 – Reminder

 You can never be too diligent about picking/ cleaning your horses feet out.

 The key here is frequency! Whether removing your horse from the stall, bringing him in from the paddock, at the in-gate or before putting back in the stall – always pick out the hooves at these times. Also ensure you apply Coppertox at least once a weak to prevent Thrush.

134 – P<small>EDICURE</small>

 Applying hoof care product on the hoof wall only and for cosmetic reasons isn't getting the job done.

 It is important to apply the hoof care product up and under the hairline, around the Coronet Band and to the heel. The job of the hoof care product is to promote foot growth and these are the areas where growth occurs. Growth does not occur at the wall of the hoof. The cosmetic use of hoof care products is secondary to the purpose of these products.

135 – TRACTOR PULL

 Never attempt to pull a loose shoe off your horse. Even if there is only a single nail remaining, you need to proceed very carefully and preferably not at all.

 Remember that properly installed shoes involve the nails being cinched backward and into the wall of the foot. Pulling down on the shoe can easily pull part of the wall of the foot off. There can be serious damage resulting from this. Always have some duct tape available to secure the shoe in the event it becomes loose and make sure you get a farrier to attend to this situation as soon as possible.

136 – Wounded

 Do not turn out a horse if he has a missing shoe.

 Hard ground can easily break up a bare and tender foot, leaving your horse lame in very short order. Always cover the foot with duct tape and then in the stall, ensure there is lots of bedding to cushion the foot while waiting for the Farrier.

137 – BED OF NAILS

 When you notice there is a missing shoe on a horse, make every effort to locate it.

 A lost shoe located somewhere in a paddock or ring is an easy object for other horses to step on and become lame, as nails and clips can penetrate the sole. Locating the missing shoe is a safety precaution and it can save you money when the Farrier puts it back on rather than charging for a new shoe.

138 – SHOELESS

 Riding your horse hard or jumping when it is due to be reset and has low foot angle is a recipe for soft tissue injury and foot/heel bruising.

 Have your horse reset regularly and don't work it hard when the farrier is due and the shoe is loose or angled low.

139 – FEET FIRST

 Ignoring hard or soft feet is always wrong. The feet need attention.

 Remember the old saying "No foot, no horse". When the footing is hard always protect your horse's sole with medicated hoof packing to ensure the sole remains soft for his comfort. If the sole becomes too soft from a moist environment you can paint the sole with different products to encourage some hardening of the sole and protect it from further moisture.

140 – ALL CORKED UP

Do not allow your horse to be flat shod while showing on grass or slippery footing or leading him to the paddock on icy paths.

Have your horse shod so that a larger sized cork can be inserted to provide traction when needed. Be sure to remove this cork and replace it with a small filler cork for the night because if you don't, the larger cork can easily cut your horse when he beds down.

Chapter VI
From The Veterinarian

141 – KEEPING SMILING

 Don't forget to make your horse's Dentist's appointment.

 Proper dental care helps your horse to chew his food properly and stay soft in the bridle. Having the teeth checked twice a year is recommended.

142 – GONE FISHING

 Not worming your horse regularly is unwise and unhealthy.

 Worms can cause drastic, sudden weight loss and can lead to a host of other ailments including colic. It is critical that your Veterinarian checks your horse regularly for worms. Ask your Veterinarian to suggest a preventative maintenance schedule (frequency of treatment) as it relates to de-worming your horse.

143 – Go There

 Do not leave your horse's sheath unattended.

 Failure to clean this area regularly can be of great discomfort to your horse and lead to larger health issues after a short while.

144 – WHAT'S UP DOC

WHAO Not disclosing current medical information to a Veterinarian during a show can have disastrous results.

GALLOP Always be aware of the medication and dosages your horse is being administered particularly when you are showing. Should your horse require Veterinary attention during a show it is critical that you share this information with the Veterinarian so that the correct medication can be applied. Firstly, many medications do not interact well and there can be unwelcome side effects if the appropriate combination of medication is not implemented. Some medications can render others ineffective as well. Secondly, there are specific medications that are not permitted for use during show time and specific allowable levels of other medications which are controlled by the shows' governing bodies. These medical regulations are strictly enforced and a violation (even if it is an accidental violation) can result in temporary disqualification and fines to a life time disqualification.

145 – Best Before

 Do not use eye creams or other topical medications that are out-dated.

 Always check the expiry date on all of your medications before applying them to your horse… better yet, check with your Veterinarian if you have any doubts.

146 – MIXING COCKTAILS

 Don't give your horse Dexamethasone with Banamine or Butazone – it will give him stomach ulcers.

 Protect your horse from the stress of showing by using a good stomach protectant such as Omeprazole.

147 – THE WORKS

 Feeding multiple supplements because they are recommended by a friend or they are the trend. This can unbalance your horse's nutrition…

 Rely on classic principles of good equine nutrition, the cornerstone being good hay and let an expert such as a vet or nutritionist tell you what else your horse may need. Feed analysis and or blood testing for specific nutrient levels can assist you in this process.

148 – MAD SCIENTIST

 Trainers giving a client horse drugs the owners don't know about without educating the owner about the risks, benefits and side effects.

 It is critical that the trainer, the vet and the owner of the horse are aware of all medications and their relationship to the animal's overall well being as well as its performance.

149 – HI HO SILVER

 Taking your horse out for a gallop or hard work out after a few days off.

 Take at least one day to warm up your horses muscles with a long slow workout after a rest. Use long walks as a fitness exercise.

150 – Salt Water

 Not paying attention to the amount of water your horse is drinking, especially in cold weather, can lead to colic and dehydration.

 Always have water of moderate temperature available to your equine and when needed add water to feeds such as beet pulp and bran mashes to ensure hydration and proper bowel function.

151 – Wrong End

 Not having a medical thermometer in the barn.

 Being able to take your horse's temperature and pulse and read its vital signs such as colour and hydration can tell you how sick it really is. Attach the thermometer to a long string so that it can hang on a hook and can be easily located, as well as removed from the rectum.

152 – Day Pass

 Do not forget your horse needs to get out regularly. Too much stall time can lead to colic and behavioral vices.

 Regular exercise significantly decreases colic and vices and increases fitness through walking. A half day in the paddock is considered minimal and a full day is recommended for most show horses. Please note that loafing sheds in the paddock will make this outside time more of a probability. Your horse will also be quieter and easier to train.

Heads Up !

Chapter VII
RANDY ROY'S CUT OUTS

RANDY ROY'S TOP BARN AND HOME RULES
(tear or cut out along the dotted line)

1. NO SMOKING IN THE BARN OR WITHIN 50' OF THE BARN

2. DOGS SHOULD BE TIED UP OR ON A LEASH (OR LEFT IN A VEHICLE WITH THE WINDOWS DOWN). BETTER STILL – LEFT AT HOME

3. CLOSE LATCHES ON STALL DOORS BEFORE LEADING A HORSE IN OR OUT

4. LET YOUR HORSE KNOW YOU ARE THERE. TALK TO HIM OR GENTLY PET HIM

5. DO NOT TRY TO DUCK UNDER THE CROSS-TIES WITH ANOTHER HORSE TO PASS IN THE AISLE

6. TURN HORSE AROUND TO FACE YOU BOTH INTO THE PADDOCK AND THE STALL BEFORE LETTING GO

7. ALWAYS MAKE SURE THE LEADSHANK AND THE HALTER ARE DONEUP WHEN LEADING A HORSE ANYWHERE

8. NO NYLON HALTERS FOR TURNOUT

9. WET THE AISLE BEFORE SWEEPING

10. ALWAYS UNDO LEG STRAPS AND SURCINGLES ON BLANKETS PRIOR TO UNDOING THE FRONT BUCKLES

RANDY ROY'S TOP BARN AND HOME RULES
(tear or cut out along the dotted line)

11. ALWAYS TAKE THE HARROWS OUT OF THE RIDING RING WHEN NOT IN USE

12. ALWAYS CHECK THE STITCHING ON YOUR TACK

13. NEVER RIDE OR JUMP ALONE

14. TRY TO EMPTY MUCK BUCKETS ON A REGULAR BASIS TO KEEP THE FLIES DOWN

15. KEEP FANS AND THEIR CORDS OUT OF THE HORSE'S REACH

16. ALWAYS MAKE SURE YOU RUN YOUR STIRRUPS UP IMMEDIATELY AFTER DISMOUNTING AND BEFORE LEADING A TACKED HORSE ANYWHERE

17. PICK OUT THE HORSE'S FEET BEFORE AND AFTER EXERCISE

18. NO COMBS OR HARSH BRUSHES SHOULD BE USED ON THE TAILS

19. ALWAYS HANG SCISSORS ON A HOOK

20. WALK FOR AT LEAST 5 MINUTES PRIOR TO GOING TO WORK AND AFTER WORK – ESPECIALLY AFTER A HARD WORKOUT

21. CRISS CROSS THE LEG STRAPS ON BLANKETS

tear or cut out along dotted line

RANDY ROY'S TOP SHOW RULES
(tear or cut out along the dotted line)

1. CONTACT NUMBERS FOR THE TRAINER AND GROOM SHOULD BE LOCATED ON A BOARD IN THE GROOMING STALL OR ON THE STALL DOORS WHERE THEY ARE EASILY VISIBLE IN CASE OF AN EMERGENCY

2. ALL DOGS SHOULD BE ON A LEASH OR TIED UP – EVEN LEFT AT HOME IF POSSIBLE

3. NO LUNGING IN A HALTER, CARRY A LUNGE WHIP AND WEAR GLOVES

4. KEEP ALL HOOKS OUT OF HORSE'S REACH

5. MAKE SURE TO USE A BREAKAWAY TIE OR KNOT WHEN TYING HORSE IN THE STALL

6. ALWAYS MAKE SURE THE LEADSHANK AND THE HALTER ARE DONE UP WHEN LEADING A HORSE ANYWHERE

7. ALWAYS UNDO LEG STRAPS AND SURCINGLES ON BLANKETS PRIOR TO UNDOING THE FRONT BUCKLES

8. CHECK STALLS FOR NAILS AND FOREIGN OBJECTS PRIOR TO PUTTING THE HORSE IN

tear or cut out along dotted line

RANDY ROY'S TOP SHOW RULES
(tear or cut out along the dotted line)

9. MAKE SURE TO REMOVE EAR PLUGS AFTER YOU HAVE FINISHED SHOWING

10. DON'T TRUST ANYONE – MAKE SURE **YOU** KNOW YOUR COURSE AND THE JUMP NUMBERS

11. KEEP FANS AND THEIR CORDS OUT OF THE HORSE'S REACH

12. ALWAYS MAKE SURE YOU RUN YOUR STIRRUPS UP IMMEDIATELY AFTER DISMOUNTING AND BEFORE LEADING A TACKED HORSE ANYWHERE

13. DO NOT USE NAILS TO HANG TACK OR HALTERS ON

14. DO NOT LEAVE STEP LADDERS OR ANY OTHER ITEMS AWAY FROM THE WALL OR UNSECURED IN A GROOMING STALL WITH A HORSE IN IT

15. NO COMBS OR HARSH BRUSHES SHOULD BE USED ON THE TAILS

16. ALWAYS HANG SCISSORS ON A HOOK AND NEVER IN A BALE

17. HAVE YOU WALKED AND GRAZED YOUR HORSE TODAY?

RANDY ROY'S TOP FARRIER RULES
(tear or cut out along the dotted line)

1. DO NOT USE TOO MUCH HOOF OIL AND DO NOT USE IT TOO OFTEN

2. HOOF OINTMENTS ARE NEEDED UNDER THE HAIRLINE AND COMPLETELY AROUND THE ENTIRE FOOT

3. DO NOT TRY TO PULL OFF A LOOSE SHOE

4. ALWAYS TRY TO FIND A LOST SHOE

5. NO HARD WORKOUTS WHEN A HORSE IS DUE TO BE SHOD

6. DO NOT TURN A HORSE OUT OR WORK THE HORSE WITH A MISSING SHOE

7. COVER THE FOOT WITH DUCT TAPE WHEN A SHOE IS LOST AND KEEP IT COVERED UNTIL THE BLACKSMITH ARRIVES

8. USE HOOF PACKING ON HARD SOLES

9. PAINT SOLES WHEN SOFT

tear or cut out along dotted line

RANDY ROY'S TOP VET RULES
(tear or cut out along the dotted line)

1. ALWAYS BANDAGE TENDONS IN

2. ALWAYS CHECK WITH THE VET WITH RESPECT TO MEDICATIONS AND SHOWING

3. KEEP ALL MEDICATIONS, SYRINGES, AND NEEDLES IN A SECURE AND LOCKED LOCATION OR CONTAINER

4. MAKE SURE TO INFORM YOUR VETERINARIAN WHAT MEDICATIONS YOUR HORSE IS SHOWING ON

5. ALWAYS HAVE A THERMOMETER WITH A STRING ATTACHED HANDY

6. ALWAYS CONSULT YOU VETERINARIAN BEFORE TRYING NEW MEDICATIONS OR DRUGS OR ANY COMBINATIONS THEREOF

tear or cut out along dotted line

RANDY ROY'S TOP VAN RULES
(tear or cut out along the dotted line)

1. ALWAYS MAKE SURE YOUR SHIPPING HALTER IS SECURE

2. MAKE SURE ALL TIES ARE BREAKABLE

3. MAKE SURE TIES ARE LONG ENOUGH TO REACH HAY AND WATER

4. MAKE SURE THE TIE IS SHORT ENOUGH THAT YOUR HORSE IS NOT FIGHTING WITH HIS NEIGHBOURS

5. MAKE SURE THE HAY NET OR HAY BAG IS FULL

6. MAKE SURE THAT WATER IS ACCESSIBLE

7. HAVE ENOUGH BEDDING TO ENCOURAGE URINATION

8. TRAILER SHOULD HAVE SUFFICIENT VENTILATION

9. BLANKETS SHOULD BE SECURE – BUT PREFERABLY OFF

10. WRAP SECURELY AND PREFERABLY NOT BEHIND

tear or cut out along dotted line

RANDY ROY'S TOP VAN RULES
(tear or cut out along the dotted line)

11. ENSURE THAT ALL RAMPS ARE UP AND SECURE

12. ENSURE THAT ALL LIGHTS ARE WORKING AND THE BRAKE CONNECTOR IS ON

13. RAMPS SHOULD HAVE MATTING TO AVOID SLIPPING

tear or cut out along dotted line

Heads Up !

RANDY ROY'S COURSE CHART
(tear or cut out along the dotted line)

PONY DISTANCES

	Small Ponies			Medium Ponies			Large Ponies			
1	19'/ 20'			21' / 22'			23' / 24'			
2	29' / 30'			31'6" / 32'			34' / 34'6"			
	Small			Medium			Large			
	Steady	Normal	Flowing	Steady	Normal	Flowing	Steady	Normal	Flowing	Forward
	9'9"	10'	10'3"	10'3"	10'6"	10'9"	11'	11'3"	11'6"	11'9"
3	39'	40'	41'	41'	42'	43'	44'	44'5"	46'	47'
4	48'9"	50'	51'3"	51'3"	52'6"	53'9"	55'	56'3"	57'6"	58'9"
5	58'6"	60'	61'6"	61'6"	63'	64'6"	66'	67'6"	69'	70'6"
6	68'3"	70'	71'9"	71'9"	73'6"	75'3"	77'	78'9"	80'6"	82'3"
7	78'	80'	82'	82'	84'	86'	88'	90'	92'	94'
8	87'9"	90'	92'3"	92'3"	94'6"	96'9"	99'	101'3"	103'6"	105'9"

RANDY ROY'S COURSE CHART
(tear or cut out along the dotted line)

HORSE DISTANCES

	3'		3'6"		3'9"		4'	
1	25'6"		26'		26'6"		27'	
2	36'6"		37'		37'6"		38'	
	12'	12'3"	12'6"	12'9"	13'	13'3"	13'6"	13'9"
3	48'	48'9"	49'6"	50'3"	51'	51'9"	52'6"	53'3"
4	60'	61'	62'	63'	64'	65'	66'	67'
5	72'	73'3"	74'6"	75'9"	77'	78'3"	79'6"	80'9"
6	84'	85'6"	87'	88'6'"	90'	91'6"	93'	94'6"
7	96'	97'9"	99'6"	101'3"	103'	104'9"	106'6"	108'3"
8	108'	110'	112'	114'	116'	118'	120'	122'

tear or cut out along dotted line

171

RANDY ROY'S STALL BOARD
ERASABLE BOARD
ITEMS – INSTRUCTIONS
(tear or cut out along the dotted line)

- NAME
- WET HAY
- WATER OFF
- VET TODAY
- FARRIER TODAY
- STALL REST
- TO SHOW
- POLOS
- HAY NET
- HAND WALK
- LUNGE
- TRIM
- BODY CLIP
- BRAN MASH

LUCKY

tear or cut out along dotted line

RANDY ROY'S DAILY SHOW CHART BOARD
HORSES NAME
(tear or cut out along the dotted line)

LUCKY

BRAID MANE ONLY

BRAID MANE AND TAIL

DIVISION SHOWING IN

FLAT AM

LESSON - TIME

SHOW - TIME

HANDWALK - TIME

LUNGE - TIME

TRAIL RIDE

tear or cut out along dotted line

RANDY ROY'S DAILY GROOM CHART -
HORSE SHOW
(tear or cut out along the dotted line)

		UPON ARRIVAL
		CHECK ALL HORSES
		STRAIGHTEN BLANKETS
		CHECK WATER
		HAY (PUT UNDER WATER PAIL)
		GRAIN - CLEAN ALL MIXING PAILS
		- REMIX ANYTHING NEEDED FOR NEXT FEEDING
		MUCK
		CLEAN WATER PAILS AND GIVE FRESH WATER
		RAKE OR SWEEP
		ORGANIZE AND CLEAN : ALL TRUNKS, RUBBERMAIDS, FEED TUBS, ETC.

		BEFORE LEAVING
		ORGANIZE AND SWEEP GROOMING STALLS
		EMPTY TACK CLEANING AND GARBAGE PAILS
		EMPTY MUCK TUBS
		CHECK WATER
		CHECK HORSES
		STRAIGHTEN BLANKETS
		LOCK DOORS

		NIGHT CHECK
		CHECK ALL HORSES
		MAKE SURE BANDAGES ARE IN PLACE
		WATER IF NEEDED
		HAY
		LOCK ALL DOORS

tear or cut out along dotted line

RANDY ROY'S DAILY CHART
(tear or cut out along the dotted line)

Name	Mon	Tues	Wed	Thur	Fri	Sat	Sun
Lucky	H/W	T/O	R	L	T	H.S.	LU

SYMBOLS	INTERPRETATION
R	RIDE
S	SCHOOL
L	LESSON
D/O	DAY OFF
GM	GROOM
LU	LUNGE
H.S.	HORSE SHOW
T	TRAIL RIDE
T/O	TURN OUT
H/W	HAND WALK
GE	GRAZE
C	CHASE
S/R	STALL REST

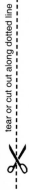

tear or cut out along dotted line

175

RANDY ROY'S DAILY GROOMING CHART
(tear or cut out along the dotted line)

GROOMING

PICK FEET / CHECK LEGS

CURRY

VACUUM IF NEEDED

LONG BRISTLE BRUSH

SOFT BRUSH

SPONGE: EYES, NOSE, UNDER TAILS, EARS

COMB MANE AND WET MANE OVER

LISTERINE TOP OF TAIL AND COMB

SHOW SHEEN AND BRUSH TAIL

TOWEL: HEAD, BODY, LEGS

DO MEDS: SEE WHITE BOARD

SHAKE OUT AND BRUSH OFF BLANKET

MANES: BRAID IF NEEDED

QUICK GROOMING

PICK FEET / CHECK LEGS

"HOT TOWEL" - HEAD, BODY, LEGS

SPONGE: EYES, NOSE, UNDER TAILS

tear or cut out along dotted line

RANDY ROY'S DAILY GROOMING CHART
(tear or cut out along the dotted line)

QUICK GROOMING (continued)

- COMB MANE AND WET MANE OVER
- LISTERINE TOP OF TAIL AND COMB
- SHOW SHEEN AND BRUSH TAIL
- DO MEDS: SEE WHITE BOARD
- TOWEL: HEAD, BODY, LEGS
- SHAKE OUT AND BRUSH OFF BLANKET

RANDY ROY'S WEEKLY GROOM CHART
(tear or cut out along the dotted line)

- CLEAN BRUSHES
- CLEAN ALL GROOMING SHELF JARS, ETC.
- CLEAN HALTERS
- COPPERTOX, PAINT CLEAN OFF
- CLEAN CONTAINERS
- VASELINE CHESTNUTS
- CHECK SADDLES, BRIDLES, GIRTHS FOR REPAIRS

tear or cut out along dotted line

Summary

WOW! I never thought I would get to 153 when I started this book. I thought maybe 50 tops and then I got to 100 and now ending up with 153 !

And ... what a ride! We have arrived at the best tip of all !

153 – BONDING

Not developing a genuine and trusting relationship with your horse guarantees unfulfilled performances.

This is arguably the most critical tip of all. You can be the most knowledgeable horse person around, but without establishing a trusting bond with your horse he will not give you his all. There needs to be a reciprocal sense of respect and gratitude established and maintained to accomplish your goals. Someone once said "a horse doesn't care how much you know until he knows how much you care".

I hope you have enjoyed them as much as I have enjoyed writing them and hoping they can help you in some way.

Thank you for letting me into your horse journeys !

Also available from Randy G. Roy